David and Mephibosheth

By Neville Stephens

I0159376

ISBN: 978-1-78364-641-8

First published in 2020

www.obt.org.uk

****

THE OPEN BIBLE TRUST
Fordland Mount, Upper Basildon,
Reading, RG8 8LU, UK

David and Mephibosheth

Contents

Introduction.. 5

Background 7

Sixteen Years Later 12

Mephibosheth was Called by the King 18

Did Mephibosheth later betray David? 26

Some final thoughts 33

About the author.. 39

Other Old Testament People 40

New Testament People... 42

Introduction

Have you ever heard of Mephibosheth? He is certainly not one of the names that come readily to mind when you think of some of the great characters from the Old Testament. But in the emotional and delightful account of this young man we see an epic story and a depiction of God's free and amazing grace in Christ to every believer today. However, before we move into this marvellous moment from the magnificent memorials of Scripture, we need to fill in some of the background to this account which has stood the test of time and is still marvelled at today by the real students of Holy Writ.

Background

Mephibosheth was the son of Jonathan, and the grandson of Saul, the first King of Israel. According to the Biblical narrative, Mephibosheth was five years old when both his father and grandfather died at the battle of Mount Gilboa (2 Samuel 4:4). After the deaths of Saul and Jonathan, Mephibosheth's nurse took him away and fled in panic. In her haste, the child fell, or was dropped while fleeing. He became lame in both of his feet, and after that, being a cripple, he was unable to walk.

His name in Hebrew is מְפִיבֹשֶׁת *Mefivoshet (Wikipedia)* meaning "from the mouth of shame", or "one who scatters and disperses shame" according to S.R. Driver. So, this poor and destitute fellow did not easily find favour with man. After his horrendous accident, we learn that he moved away and that he journeyed seeking refuge, which he found "at the house of Makir, son of Ammiel in Lo Debar" (2 Samuel 9:4).

Lo Debar was a town in Gilead not far from Mahanaim and north of the Jabbok river. In Hebrew it means "no pasture" or "no communication", and it was considered a very lowly place to live in Biblical times. Also, Makir means "sold", so on the face of it, Mephibosheth did not have an awful lot going for him. However, in Lo Debar, despite his physical condition, he found grace in the eyes of an un-named woman whom he married according to the writings of Josephus. We know from Scripture that with his new bride he was able to father at least one child, a son called Mika or Micah.

After this, his fortunes began to improve somewhat, and a little later he was to find that he had a lot going for him. For in the hidden realms of heavenly glory the Lord had plans for him, and the fortunes of this disabled character were soon to change quite dramatically.

During the reign of David there was a time when his countrymen suffered a famine for three successive years. And when the King sought the face of the Lord for the reason for this judgement, he was informed that "it was on account of Saul and his blood-stained house, and it is because he put the Gibeonites to death" (2 Samuel 21:1).

The Gibeonites were not actually part of Israel, but they were survivors from the Amorites whom the Israelites had sworn to spare. However, the treacherous and sinful Saul, in his zeal for Israel and Judah, broke this promise and attempted to annihilate the Gibeonites!

When David heard that the atrocity was against the Gibeonites, the hairs on his neck must have stood on end and a cold chill run down his spine! He knew they were really *not* the people for Saul to attack and kill. For in the days of Joshua, more than 400 years before David's time,

Israel swore not to harm the neighbouring tribe of the Gibeonites (Joshua 9).

God expected Israel to keep its promise, even though the Gibeonites tricked Israel into making the agreement. Therefore, Saul's crime was not only in killing the Gibeonites, but rather, and more importantly, it was the breaking of this ancient and important oath. Such covenants and oaths are solemn to the Lord for Israel then, and similarly His promises for us today. And He is not amused when they are taken lightly.

This emphasises some very important principles. God expects us to keep our promises. God expects nations to keep their promises as well. Time does not diminish our obligation to such promises. God's correction may come a long time after the offence. But if God has such a high expectation that the people of Israel keep their covenants and that He will reward them, then we can have total confidence and assurance that He will keep His promises to us, and especially the guarantee of salvation found in the Lord Jesus Christ.

So David sought to reach a peaceful resolution with the Gibeonites. But even though Saul made a wholesale slaughter of this people in his outrageous attack upon them, they did not ask for the same among the people of Israel. Instead of an eye for an eye, they just sought revenge against the household of Saul and his descendants, and David agreed to this.

In a generous act of appeasement, David asked the leaders of this severely depleted and decimated nation what he could do for them to make some sort of amends to them, for his nation breaking their promises to them. The Gibeonites did not ask for gold or silver or any treasure trove, but what they did ask for was revenge against Saul. They asked that his seven sons be handed over to them to be executed in an act of vengeance and justice.

David agreed to this, even though the terms of death were to be a long-protracted set of hangings (some commentators even say "crucifixions") lasting several months leading up to "the first days of the harvest, just as the barley harvest was beginning" (verses 1-9). However, towards the end of this narrative, we are told that "the king spared Mephibosheth, the son of Jonathan, the son of Saul, because of the oath before the Lord between David and Jonathan, the son of Saul" (v. 7).

> So the king took Armoni and Mephibosheth, the two sons of Rizpah the daughter of Aiah, whom she bore to Saul; and the five sons of Michal the daughter of Saul, whom she brought up for Adriel the son of Barzillai the Meholathite; and he delivered them into the hands of the Gibeonites,

and they hanged them on the hill before the LORD. So they fell, all seven together, and were put to death in the days of harvest, in the first days, in the beginning of barley harvest. (2 Samuel 21:7-9)

So, we have a sacrifice of perfection (v. 7), leading to the cleansing of the land, and it took place around the time of the Passover (beginning of barley harvest).

Then they hanged them on the hill before the Lord. David chose seven male descendants of Saul to give over to the Gibeonites and they executed them by public hanging. The phrase "before the LORD" implies that God approved of their execution, similar to the slaughter by Joshua, on the command of the Lord, of the people of Jericho (Joshua 6:21). Our holy and righteous God can approve of things which appear horrendous to us on the surface.

The method of death was also important because it fulfilled the promise of Deuteronomy 21:22-23 "that anyone who is hung on a tree is under God's curse". These descendants of Saul bore the curse Saul deserved and so delivered Israel from the guilt of their sin against the Gibeonites. This promise from Deuteronomy explains why Jesus died the way He did and why He was buried the same day. Galatians 3:13 explains that Christ has redeemed the curse of the law having become a curse Himself.

Sixteen Years Later

Sixteen years have now passed since David made a covenant with Jonathan, but now the time had arrived for the King to fulfil his covenant promise to his former beloved companion, and to honour the pact. We read that Jonathan said: "But show me unfailing kindness like the LORD's kindness as long as I live, so that I may not be killed, and do not ever cut off your kindness from my family—not even when the LORD has cut off every one of David's enemies from the face of the earth." So Jonathan made a covenant with the house of David, saying, "May the LORD call David's enemies to account." And Jonathan had David reaffirm his oath out of love for him, because he loved him as he loved himself (1 Samuel 20:14-17).

So here we are many years later, as David sought out the last survivor of his dear friend and companion (2 Samuel 9). David sent for Mephibosheth, and brought him to the palace. When Mephibosheth first learned that the king had found him, he must have been terrified. He knew what had become of Saul's sons. Fearful and trembling, he came into David's presence, expecting to be slain. What a blessed surprise he found! David showed him nothing but kindness and mercy. He was made to be as one of the king's sons.

Does this not offer us a superb illustration of the real gospel of Jesus, and how He calls the undeserving to meet Him and then to be blessed? Behind the majestic and generously kind consideration of David toward Mephibosheth, the gregarious grace of God towards us shines forth brilliantly.

When the poor, crippled son of Jonathan was brought from Lo Debar to Jerusalem, and made to sit at the king's table, I am sure that he was lost in bewilderment and amazement. And when a servant of sin like us is made a saint and a joint-heir with Christ, we too are lost in amazing and wonderful love for our Saviour and King. As the songwriter eulogises:

> All Heaven declares
> The glory of the risen Lord.
> Who can compare
> With the beauty of the Lord?
> Forever you will be
> The Lamb upon the throne.
> I gladly bow the knee
> And worship you alone.
>
> I will proclaim
> The glory of the risen Lord.
> Who once was slain
> To reconcile man to God.
> Forever you will be

The Lamb upon the throne.
I gladly bow the knee
And worship you alone.

David's kindness to Mephibosheth for Jonathan's sake is a beautiful picture of God's lovingkindness and tender mercy to sinners like us for Christ's sake. As we go through this narrative, there are many things which stand out about this poor prince Mephibosheth, and they illustrate vividly the grace of God to us in Christ.

When David sought him out, Mephibosheth was in a very miserable condition and was totally unworthy of the attention of the King. But David freely showed kindness and mercy to him and we, too, are unworthy to receive anything from God. Nevertheless, He is gracious to us.
Mephibosheth was poor, destitute, helpless and living in a hillbilly backwater named "Lo Debar"! And that just about summed up the condition we were in before we met Christ.

> All of us have become like one who is unclean, and all our righteous acts are like filthy rags. We all shrivel up like a leaf, and like the wind our sins sweep us away. No one calls on your name or strives to lay hold of you, for you have hidden your face from us and have given us over to our sins. (Isaiah 64: 6-7)

From the sole of our foot to the top of our head, there is no soundness in us, only wounds and welts and open sores, not cleansed or bandaged or soothed with oil. (Isaiah 1:6)

"Our righteous acts are like filthy rags" (Isaiah 64:6) is as lowly and as dirty an expression one can use, if you take the time to research the real meaning behind this selected phrase. We were menstrual throwaways, discards on a par with the leper or the prostitute – such was our condition before Christ met us and thoroughly cleansed us of such impurities! Mephibosheth means "a shameful thing" in heart, will and deed and we were all Mephibosheths before Jesus entered our lives.

Another point to remember in this sensational story is that Mephibosheth was the king's enemy. He was the grandson of the unholy and blood-stained Saul, and therefore was a natural enemy to David. He was hiding from the King. However, David was not his enemy. By nature, we are all enemies of God because we are all sons and daughters of Adam.

The sinful mind is hostile to God. It does not submit to God's law, nor can it do so. Those controlled by the sinful nature cannot please God. (Romans 8:7-8)

We were sinners and hiding from God when He saved us. But God is not the enemy of His people, He invites us in, for He loves us!

Moving on then we can note that the young prince became lame through a fall.

> Jonathan son of Saul had a son who was lame in both feet. He was five years old when the news about Saul and Jonathan came from Jezreel. His nurse picked him up and fled, but as she hurried to leave, he fell and became disabled. His name was Mephibosheth. (2 Samuel 4:4)

As we progress to chapter nine, we are looking at events some sixteen years later after the oath between David and Jonathan.

> David asked, "Is there anyone still left of the house of Saul to whom I can show kindness for Jonathan's sake?" Now there was a servant of Saul's household named Ziba. They summoned him to appear before David, and the king said to him, "Are you Ziba?" "At your service," he replied. The king asked, "Is there no one still alive from the house of Saul to whom I can show God's kindness?" Ziba answered the king, "There is still a son of Jonathan; he is lame in both feet." "Where is he?" the king asked. Ziba answered, "He is at the

house of Makir son of Ammiel in Lo Debar." So King David had him brought from Lo Debar, from the house of Makir son of Ammiel. (2 Samuel 9:1-5)

At his birth, Mephibosheth was not a cripple physically, only spiritually like all of us. God created our first parents sinless or "God created mankind upright but they have gone in search of many schemes" (Ecclesiastes 7:29). From helpful, we became helpless through the fall of our father Adam.

We can also note in this passage, in verse four of 2 Samuel 9, that Mephibosheth seemed to be hiding in a far distant place, for not many people would want to live in the despised Lo Debar, as it was an undesirable place to situate oneself. Therefore, he was far away from the king. He was far away from Jerusalem. He was far away from the place of peace. He was far away from the place of worship. He was in the house of Makir which means "sold", and he was down in Lo Debar, the place of "no substance or communication".

This was our condition by nature, until Christ entered our lives. We were lost and very far from the Lord. We were sold under sin and far away from the Salvation found in Jesus. We were in a barren desert place with no "real bread or substance" until we found the true "Bread of Life" (John 6:35).

Mephibosheth was Called by the King

The fortunes of the desolate young prince are about to be set on the pathway to improvement. "Where is he?" the king asked. Ziba answered, "He is at the house of Makir son of Ammiel in Lo Debar." So King David had him brought from Lo Debar, from the house of Makir son of Ammiel" (2 Samuel 9:4-5).

David sought Mephibosheth and brought him to the palace. Here, again, we see God's marvellous grace towards sinners. He seeks His own sheep. And when He finds His sheep, He brings it home, as in:

> Then Jesus told them this parable: "Suppose one of you has a hundred sheep and loses one of them. Doesn't he leave the ninety-nine in the open country and go after the lost sheep until he finds it? And when he finds it, he joyfully puts it on his shoulders and goes home. Then he calls his friends and neighbours together and says, 'Rejoice with me; I have found my lost sheep. I tell you that in the same way there will be more rejoicing in heaven over one sinner who repents than over ninety-nine righteous persons who do not need to repent." (Luke 15:3-7; also note the similarities in the parable of the lost son, Luke 15:11-32).

So we see that David sought Mephibosheth – the young lame prince did not seek the king. It was a sovereign choice, and it was a personal call by the monarch.

> Blessed are those you choose and bring near to live in your courts! We are filled with the good things of your house, of your holy temple. You answer us with awesome 'and righteous deeds, God our Saviour, the hope of all the ends of the earth and of the farthest seas (Psalm 65:4-5).

Salvation begins with God. He takes the initiative. Man goes astray. Man hides from God. But the Lord seeks and finds His own. And once found they will never be lost.

God almighty sends His Spirit to seek and find His people, who have strayed far away from Him. He always finds them; and He always brings them home. He instructs them to follow Him, and they duly oblige by coming to Him and remaining loyal. As Jesus said,

> "My sheep listen to my voice; I know them, and they follow me. I give them eternal life, and they shall never perish; no one will snatch them out of my hand. My Father, who has given them to me, is greater than all; no one can snatch them out of my Father's hand. I and the Father are one" (John 10: 27-30).

We will now see that Mephibosheth came before the king in reverent submission. For "when Mephibosheth son of Jonathan, the son of Saul, came to David, he bowed down to pay him honour" (2 Samuel 9:6, NIV) or "fell on his face and did reverence him" saying "Behold thy servant!" (KJV).

When he first came before David, he reverenced him with fear and trembling. He did not know what David would do with him. He could kill him, or he could let him live. So Mephibosheth threw himself at the king's feet.

Were you not like me when I first came to Christ – bowing the heart in holy submission? We throw ourselves down at the saving feet of the Master. And just as Jesus broke any fear we might have in His holy presence, likewise David did the same by calling the lame prince by name and speaking soothing and comforting words to him: "Mephibosheth, do not be afraid, for I will surely show you kindness".

Another vital assurance we can glean from this narrative is that Mephibosheth was received in all of his deformity without any improvement. David received the poor cripple as he was, and the Lord our God receives sinners like us in all of our deformities and sins.
Mephibosheth was also received for the sake of another, and this offers yet another superb depiction of how we are

received by The Father because of the sacrifice of The Son on Calvary:

> David said to him, "I will surely show you kindness for the sake of your father Jonathan. I will restore to you all of the land that belonged to your grandfather Saul and you will always eat at my table." (2 Samuel 9:7).

David received Mephibosheth altogether for Jonathan's sake, because he loved Jonathan.

On the basis of Christ's righteous obedience, as our Representative, and His voluntary death as our Substitute, God receives believing sinners. It pleases God to look on Christ and pardon all who believe on Him. Just as David received Mephibosheth because of his relationship to Jonathan, God receives us because of our relationship to Christ.

As we move on we will note that when Mephibosheth came to David, he had learned to have a proper estimate of himself even describing himself as "a dead dog" (2 Samuel 9:8). We too were like dead dogs when we came to Christ for salvation, for we were dead in our sins, and our righteousness was totally useless and like filthy rags as we have already mentioned. We have nothing of eternal merit until we meet Christ, but once we are saved, we are offered a place at His table and are to sit with Him in the heavenly places (Ephesians 2:6). Quite amazing!

Mephibosheth was also reconciled to the king by an act of the king's own mercy, and not because of anything he could bring into the palace to draw attention to himself.

> Then the king summoned Ziba, Saul's steward, and said to him, "I have given your master's grandson everything that belonged to Saul and his family. You and your sons and your servants are to farm the land for him and bring in the crops, so that your master's grandson may be provided for. And Mephibosheth, grandson of your master, will always eat at my table." Now Ziba had fifteen sons and twenty servants (2 Samuel 9:9-10).

David restored Mephibosheth and made him as one of the king's sons, a prince, just like us as God looks at us through Jesus! Amazingly, Mephibosheth received a lot more in David than he had lost in Saul. Just as we receive a lot more in Christ than we lost in sin through Adam. The Lord has given us eternal life. He has given us peace in Him. He has given us an eternal inheritance. Christ has provided for us all that we need. And in Christ we are given the highest possible honour and dignity. This is summed up for us beautifully by the Apostle Paul:

> Praise be to the God and Father of our Lord Jesus Christ, who has blessed us in the heavenly realms

with every spiritual blessing in Christ, for he chose us in him before the creation of the world to be holy and blameless in his sight. In love he predestined us for adoption to son-ship through Jesus Christ, in accordance with his pleasure and will— to the praise of his glorious grace, which he has freely given us in the one he loves. In him we have redemption through his blood, the forgiveness of sins, in accordance with the riches of God's grace that he lavished on us. With all wisdom and understanding, he made known to us the mystery of his will according to his good pleasure, which he purposed in Christ, to be put into effect when the times reach their fulfilment—to bring unity to all things in heaven and on earth under Christ. In him we were also chosen, having been predestined according to the plan of him who works out everything in conformity with the purpose of his will, in order that we, who were the first to put our hope in Christ, might be for the praise of his glory. And you also were included in Christ when you heard the message of truth, the gospel of your salvation. When you believed, you were marked in him with a seal, the promised Holy Spirit, who is a deposit guaranteeing our inheritance until the redemption of those who are God's possession—to the praise of his glory. (Ephesians 1:3-14)

And under the king's table, Mephibosheth's crippled feet were covered and not to be seen or glared at. He was still lame in both his feet, but his deformity was covered under David's table. Now, blessed be God, in Christ all the sins of His people are covered through the Blood of Jesus.

As we move on, another point to note is that Mephibosheth was granted perpetual fellowship and communion with the king. Once more the king's house was his house, just as it was previously under Saul's reign. He dwelt with David. He was always accepted in David's presence. And as children of God, it is our privilege and joy to dwell with the King now, and in the heavenly glory to come. We walk in His company now. We are allowed to speak to Him freely today and at all times. We live upon His riches, and we rest under His protection. Because of the grace he had received, the crippled prince loved the king above everything, and this delightful chapter nine concludes with him dining like the king's own, and he always ate at the king's table (2 Samuel 9:11-13).

One more thing we have to note is that all of this was done for Mephibosheth because of a covenant made before he was born. And all that we have in Christ and all that we have experienced of divine grace, has been given to us because of the love of the Father and the Son in total agreement long before we were born. Mephibosheth did not know anything about the covenant, but David did!

God our Father loves us and deals graciously with us because of Christ and our relationship with Him. Indeed, He loves us as He loves His dear Son!

So, we conclude this section by summarising and reminding ourselves that Mephibosheth was in a very miserable condition when the king sought him out. He was called by the king. He was reconciled by an act of the king's mercy. Mephibosheth was granted perpetual fellowship and communion with the king, and all of this was done for Mephibosheth, because of a covenant made long before he was born.

And this would be a very nice place to finish this moving and emotional love story, as most commentators do. Unfortunately, there is another section we must consider which sours the account a little, and one which reminds us that we are surrounded by enemies in this world. Or as Paul puts it, "for our struggle is not against flesh and blood, but against the rulers, against the authorities, against the powers of this dark world and against the spiritual forces of evil in the heavenly realms" (Ephesians 6:12), and these seek to make us lose the joy of our salvation.

Did Mephibosheth later betray David?

Sadly, all does not end as well for the rejuvenated crippled prince as it should have done, for there was an enemy in the camp and in the royal palace who despised him and wanted to see his downfall.

We know that now, just as then, all the chosen of God have a powerful enemy who can translate himself into an angel of light (2 Corinthians 11:14), who is the god of this world (2 Corinthians 4:4), who is the prince of the power of the air (Ephesians 2:2), who is the father of all lies (John 8:44), who is one stalking us like a lion wanting to devour us (1 Peter 5:8), and who is one who even still has access into the heavenly places today (Ephesians 6:12). So we should not be surprised that Satan has his devilish hand in the latter parts of our narrative to serve as a warning to all of us.

An interval of about fourteen years has now passed, and a big crisis has arrived in David's life. On this occasion we possess two accounts of Mephibosheth's behaviour, namely his own in 2 Samuel 19:24-30 but also that of Ziba in 2 Samuel 16:1-4. These are at variance with each other.

Absalom led a rebellion against his father David, and David has been driven out of Jerusalem. Ziba, David's servant, and the overseer of Mephibosheth, Jonathan's son, has cheated Mephibosheth and deserted him and left him behind with Absalom, even though he wanted to go with Ziba. The duplicitous servant Ziba lied to David and told David that Mephibosheth had been complicit with Absalom. However, Absalom was killed, and David returned to Jerusalem having heard Ziba's account, and he meets Mephibosheth whom he thinks has been a traitor.

Ziba's account was given to the king on his flight at the most opportune moment, just as David has undergone the most tiring part of that trying day's journey. He had just taken the last look at the city so peculiarly his own, and has just about completed the hot and toilsome ascent of the Mount of Olives. He was on foot, and in need of relief and refreshment. The relief and refreshment has arrived. There stood a couple of strong he-asses, ready saddled for the king or his household to make use of. There were grapes, melons and bread, and a skin of wine; and there was the donor of these welcome gifts, Ziba, with respect in his look and sympathy on his tongue.

Of course, the whole, although offered by the deceitful Ziba, was really the property of Mephibosheth. The asses are his, one of them is even his own riding animal (see 2 Chronicles 17:2, and 19:26), and the fruits are from his gardens and orchards. But why is not their owner here in person? Where is the "son of Saul"?

He, says Ziba, is in Jerusalem, waiting to receive from the nation the throne of his grandfather, that throne from which he has so long been unjustly excluded. Such an aspiration would be very natural, but it must have been speedily dissipated by the thought that he at least would be likely to gain little by Absalom's rebellion. Still it must be confessed that Ziba's tale at first sight, was a most plausible one, and that the answer of David is no more than was to be expected.

So the presumed ingratitude of Mephibosheth is requited with the ruin he deserves, while the loyalty and thoughtful courtesy of Ziba are rewarded by the possessions of his master, thus reinstating him in the position which he seems to have occupied before Mephibosheth's arrival in Judah.

Mephibosheth's story, however, which he had not the opportunity of telling until several days later, when he met David returning to his kingdom at the western bank of the Jordan, was very different from Ziba's. He had been desirous to flee with his patron and benefactor, and had ordered Ziba to make ready his ass that he might join the cortege. But Ziba had deceived him, he had left him, and had not returned with the asses. In his helpless condition he had no alternative, once the opportunity of accompanying David was lost, but to remain where he was. The swift pursuit which had been made after Ahimaaz and Jonathan (2 Samuel 17) had shown what risks even a strong and able man must run who would try to follow the king. However, all that he could do under the circumstances Mephibosheth had done: he just waited.

He had gone into the deepest mourning possible (the same as in 2 Samuel 12:20) for his lost friend. From the very day that David left he had allowed his beard to grow ragged, his crippled feet were unwashed and untended, and his clothes remained unchanged. That David did not disbelieve this story is shown by his revoking the judgment he had previously given. That he did not entirely reverse his decision, but allowed Ziba to retain possession of half the lands of Mephibosheth, is probably due partly to weariness of the whole scenario, but mainly to the conciliatory frame of mind in which he was at that moment.

"Shall, then, any man be put to death this day?" (2 Samuel 19:22) is the key note of the whole proceedings. David was doubtless touched by the devotedness of his friend's son, as well as angry at the imposition of Ziba, but perhaps he was not wholly convinced of Mephibosheth's innocence. The king makes an error of judgment here, which goes to show, once again, that David made a number of wrong decisions in his regal life despite being a godly man, and one who bore the heart of the Lord (1 Samuel 13:14 and Acts 13:22).

There was, at that point in time, no opportunity to fully examine into the matter. Also, perhaps, actuated by the pride of an already expressed judgment, or by reluctance to offend Ziba who had adhered to him when so many old friends forsook him, he answered abruptly, "Why say any more. I order you and Ziba to divide the land" (2 Samuel 19:29).

The answer of Mephibosheth was worthy of the son of the generous Jonathan, and shows that he had met a better reception than he had expected. He resolutely exclaims, "Let him take everything now that my lord the king has arrived home safely" (2 Samuel 19:30).

Now pause for a moment and note this amazing statement from the crippled prince. It is quite an astonishing exclamation and possibly one of the most exceptional expressions of love in all the Bible. And a beautiful prototype of how we should love Jesus - "let him take everything now that my lord the king has arrived home safely".

Mephibosheth was deserted and treated unfairly by Ziba. When David has to decide between the two, he doesn't know what to say, and so he splits the difference, which is distinctly unfair on Mephibosheth. However, in spite of all that, Mephibosheth cares nothing for the inheritance, because he loves the king so much.

So my question is this: What goes into making love like this? And I see at least five things here.

1. In the middle of verse 27: great admiration for the king. "My lord the king is like the angel of God."
2. The end of verse 27: utter submission to the king's wisdom. "David, do therefore, what seems good to you."
3. Verse 28: being amazed by grace. Mephibosheth says: "For all my father's house were but men doomed to death before my lord the king, but you set your servant among those who eat at your table." Mephibosheth had never got over the fact that he was the grandson of David's sworn enemy Saul, and David took him and made him like a son to eat at his own table. He never got over it.
4. The end of verse 28: a sense of having no rights or claims. He says: "What further right have I, then, to cry to the king?"
5. A deep sense of unworthiness and why we like the prince are all lost even to the point of being like dead dogs.

Back in 2 Samuel 9:7, David says to Mephibosheth: "Don't be afraid. For I will show you kindness for the sake of your father Jonathan. I will restore to you all the land of Saul your father and you shall eat at my table always." And to this Mephibosheth responds, "What is your servant that you should show regard for a dead dog such as I?"

How can sinners like us love a king? The answer is for us to recognise that we really were similar to dead dogs, but by the grace of God have been transformed into joint heirs with Christ and to sit at His table: praise the Lord! Friends, our debt to God is infinite. We have done far worse than Mephibosheth, yet we have been loved, and we have been set regally at the King's table.

Should we not love Jesus like Mephibosheth loved David, only more? When we are offered riches in this world — and when Jesus finally comes back and we are given rewards in the age to come — I hope that we will say to Jesus, "Oh, let somebody else take it all since my Lord the King has come safely home."

Some final thoughts

I would like to close this booklet with some final thoughts on why the Lord should choose such nondescript, nobodies and virtually unknown characters such as Mephibosheth to shine so brightly throughout the pages of Scripture. The young crippled prince had nothing to offer King David, in the same manner we come to Christ with nothing to offer of our own that has value or importance. As the Apostle Paul puts it:

> It is because of him that you are in Christ Jesus, who has become for us wisdom from God—that is, our righteousness, holiness and redemption. Therefore, as it is written: "Let the one who boasts, boast in the Lord." (1 Corinthians 1: 30-31).

The reason God does what He does is to demonstrate that He alone is the source of our salvation. "It is because of him that you are in Christ Jesus." It is not our wisdom or our intellect or our memorised Bible verses that brought us to Jesus. And we are not a Christian because we are a good person or a church member or because our father was a preacher and our mother was a Sunday school teacher. Paul says plainly: "It is because of him." Salvation is of the Lord. God wants us to know that He is the reason that we came to Christ. And in Christ we find wisdom, righteousness, holiness and redemption. If we believe this, then our boast will be in the Lord alone.

When it comes to salvation, we contribute nothing but the sin that makes it necessary to be saved. God does the rest. God chooses whom He pleases, and amazingly He often chooses those whom the world would overlook rather easily.

If we believe what this passage (1 Corinthians 1:30-31) teaches, it will change the way we look at ourselves, and it will change the way we talk about ourselves. Some of us talk so much about ourselves that we hardly talk about the Lord at all. Our real problem is the vast difference between our view and God's view.

We look at the outward.
   God looks at the inward.
We value popularity.
   God values character.
We look at intelligence.
   God looks at the heart.
We honour those with money.
   God honours those with integrity.
We talk about what we own.
   God talks about what we give away.
We boast about whom we know.
   God notices whom we serve.
We list our accomplishments.

David and Mephibosheth

God looks for a contrite heart.

We value education.

God values wisdom.

We love size and quantity.

God notices quality.

We live for fame.

God searches for humility.

Our view is shallow.

God's view is deep.

Our view is temporary.

God's view is eternal.

Consider the roll call of some of God's imperfect heroes, for the talent pool has always been pretty thin on the ground when it comes to moral perfection and, in reality, it is probably nil:

- Noah who got drunk.
- Abraham who lied about his wife.
- Jacob who was a deceiver.
- Moses who murdered an Egyptian.
- Rahab who was a harlot.
- Samson who had serious problems with lust and anger.
- David who was a murderer and an adulterer.
- Mephibosheth who was a crippled failure far away from the king.
- Onesimus who was a runaway slave.

- The thief on the cross who was crucified for his sins.
- Mary of Magdala who was demon possessed.
- James and John who wanted to bring fire down upon a Samaritan village.
- Paul who persecuted the church.
- Peter who denied Christ.

The list is endless for we could certainly add a lot more names to this outrageous list of sinners who did not deserve the grace of God – just like our sinful selves. In reality, without Christ, we are all lost and are pathetic losers. We do not know the half of it. So why does God choose splendid sinners and lovable losers? Why are there so many miserable misfits and fantastic failures in God's family? The answer is two-fold:

1. God chooses losers because that is all He has got to work with.
2. And God chooses losers because that way He alone gets the credit for anything good we accomplish.

Here is the good news. When splendid sinners, and lovable losers, and miserable misfits, and fantastic failures band together to seek the Lord, amazing things happen. The Red Sea parts, the walls come tumbling down, the enemy is routed, and the church rolls on for the glory of God.

This side of heaven, we are a pretty sorry lot, but that is where God's grace comes in. No one will be saved by what they do. Our only hope of heaven is to run to the cross and lay hold of Jesus Christ. And we will not even do that unless God helps us to do it, and even then, He must give us the strength to hang on and to keep believing. Apart from God's grace, even our best efforts are nothing more than splendid sins!

About the author

Neville Stephens is a retired Postmaster from Watford but now lives, along with his wife Hazel, in his second home, the land of his parents: South Wales. He has been associated with The Open Bible Trust for over 35 years and has spoken at a number of OBT events and has written two booklets for the OBT: *Unanswered Prayer* and *The Twelve Apostles.*

He is a blogger and is well-known for arranging Bible Prophecy Conferences, and also speaks at some of these with his PowerPoint presentations on what is happening in The Middle East, his views on the Antichrist and explaining why that he thoroughly disagrees with the popular prophetic scenario of a 'Revised Roman Empire'.

Other Old Testament People

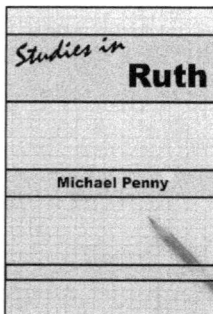

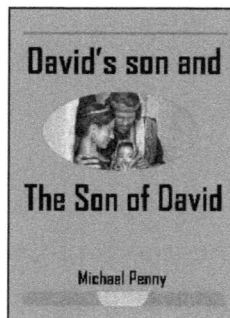

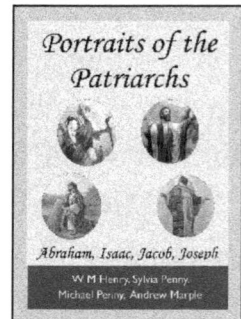

Abraham

James Poole

Isaac

James Poole

Jacob

James Poole

Joseph

James Poole

Joshua—Jesus

The Pioneer of Their Salvation

Charles Ozanne

Esther and Ruth

Charles Ozanne

Studies in **Ruth**

Michael Penny

David's son and The Son of David

Michael Penny

Portraits of the Patriarchs

Abraham, Isaac, Jacob, Joseph

W. M. Henry, Sylvia Penny, Michael Penny, Andrew Marple

Details of these can be seen on **www.obt.org.uk**
and they can be ordered from that website.

They are also available
as eBooks from Amazon and Apple
and as paperbacks from Amazon.

New Testament People

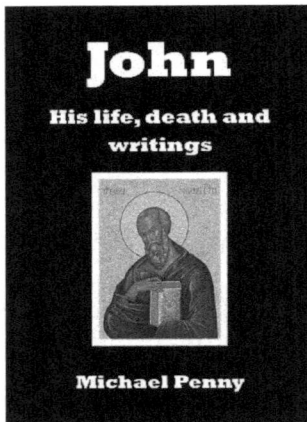

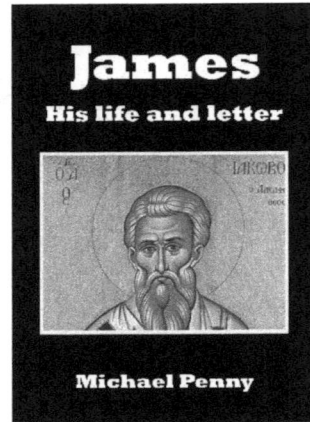

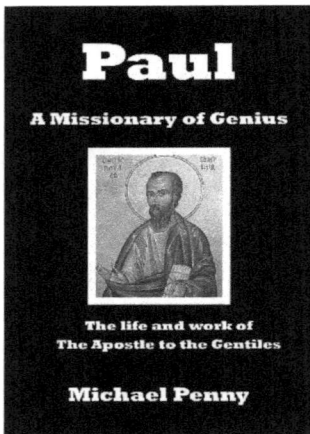

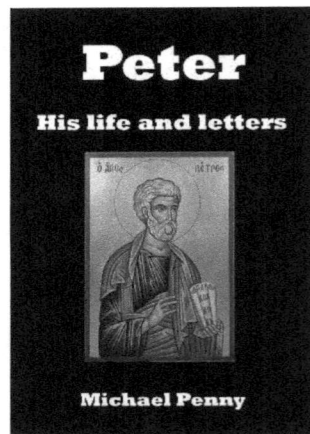

John

His life, death and writings

Michael Penny

James

His life and letter

Michael Penny

Paul

A Missionary of Genius

The life and work of
The Apostle to the Gentiles

Michael Penny

Peter

His life and letters

Michael Penny

Details of these can be seen on **www.obt.org.uk**
and they can be ordered from that website.

They are also available as
eBooks from Amazon and Apple
and as paperbacks from Amazon.

Publications of The Open Bible Trust must be in accordance with its evangelical, fundamental and dispensational basis. However, beyond this minimum, writers are free to express whatever beliefs they may have as their own understanding, provided that the aim in so doing is to further the object of The Open Bible Trust. A copy of the doctrinal basis is available on **www.obt.org.uk** or from:

THE OPEN BIBLE TRUST
Fordland Mount, Upper Basildon,
Reading, RG8 8LU, UK

www.ingramcontent.com/pod-product-compliance
Lightning Source LLC
Chambersburg PA
CBHW060632030426
42337CB00018B/3316